Bridgestone
B O O K S

World of Insects

Beetles

by Deirdre A. Prischmann

Consultant:
Gary A. Dunn, MS, Director of Education
Young Entomologists' Society Inc.
Lansing, Michigan

Bridgestone Books are published by Capstone Press,
151 Good Counsel Drive, P.O. Box 669, Mankato, Minnesota 56002.
www.capstonepress.com

Library of Congress Cataloging-in-Publication Data
Prischmann, Deirdre A.
　　Beetles / Deirdre A. Prischmann.
　　p. cm.—(Bridgestone books. World of insects)
　　Includes bibliographical references and index.
　　ISBN 0-7368-3706-X (hardcover)
　　1. Beetles—Juvenile literature. I. Title. II. Series: World of insects.
QL576.2.P75 2005
595.76—dc22   2004015228

Summary: A brief introduction to beetles, discussing their characteristics, habitat, life cycle, and
　　predators. Includes a range map, life cycle illustration, and amazing facts.

Editorial Credits
Becky Viaene, editor; Jennifer Bergstrom, designer; Erin Scott, Wylde Hare Creative, illustrator;
　　Jo Miller, photo researcher; Scott Thoms, photo editor

Photo Credits
Bill Beatty, 18
Brand X Pictures, back cover
Bruce Coleman Inc./Bob Gossington, 10; Bob Jensen, 4; Mik Dakin, 6
Dwight R. Kuhn, 16
James P. Rowan, 12, 20
Pete Carmichael, 1
Unicorn Stock Photos/R. E. Barber, cover

1 2 3 4 5 6 10 09 08 07 06 05

Table of Contents

Beetles

Did you know beetles are one of the most common insects? One of every four insects is a beetle.

Beetles are insects with hard wing covers. Insects have six legs, three body sections, and an **exoskeleton**. The exoskeleton covers an insect's body.

◄ A brightly colored striped scarab beetle crawls across a flower in Arizona.

What Beetles Look Like

There are many different kinds of beetles. Each kind looks different. Beetles can grow to be as long as a new pencil. Other beetles are so small that they are hard to see. Beetles can be black or colorful. Some have horns.

All beetles have a head, **thorax**, and **abdomen**. A beetle's head holds the eyes, mouthparts, and **antennas**. Insects use antennas to feel and smell. Beetles have four wings and six legs attached to their thorax. The thorax is connected to the abdomen.

◄ A wood-boring beetle stretches its four wings out to fly past oak flowers.

Beetle Range Map

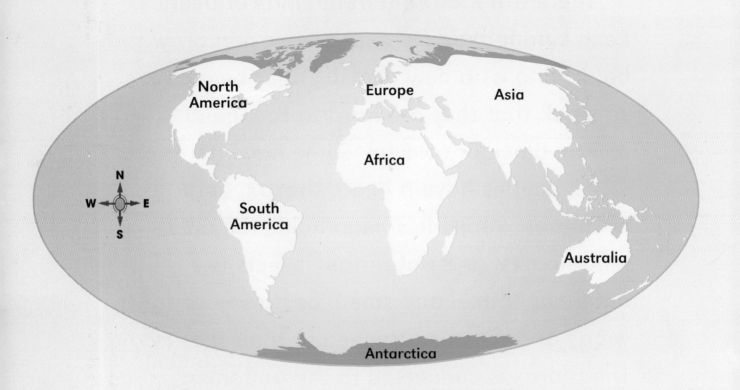

North America

Europe

Asia

Africa

South America

Australia

Antarctica

N
W   E
S

☐ Where Beetles Live

Beetles in the World

Beetles are found around the world. However, no beetles live in the very cold Antarctica and the Arctic. Most beetles live in hot places.

Many beetles move to new areas by flying. To fly, beetles lift their front wings and unfold their back wings. Some beetles can't fly. They crawl to new places.

◄ Beetles live in most parts of the world, except very cold areas.

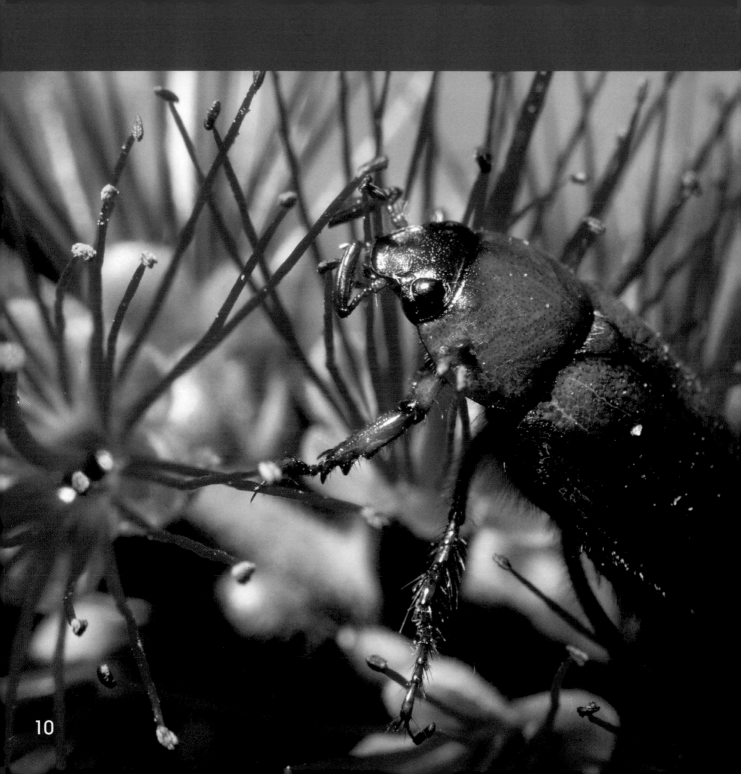

Beetle Habitats

Most beetles live on land. Some beetles live underground in dirt. Above ground, some beetles live inside plants and **fungi**. Others live inside acorns or other seeds. Beetles also crawl around inside dark caves.

Some beetles, including diving beetles, live in water. They swim and live in rivers, streams, and lakes. A few beetles can even live in hot springs. No beetles can live in salty ocean water.

◀ June beetles can often be found on plants.

What Beetles Eat

Most beetles eat plants. They eat leaves, stems, roots, flowers, and fruit off plants.

Beetles can be harmful to plants. Weevil beetles can ruin rice fields and apple trees. Potato beetles can harm large potato fields.

Some beetles eat animals. Burying beetles eat dead mice, birds, and other small animals. Some large diving beetles even eat small fish.

◄ A milkweed longhorn beetle grabs onto a flower with its legs. It uses mouthparts to cut and eat the flower.

Life Cycle of a Beetle

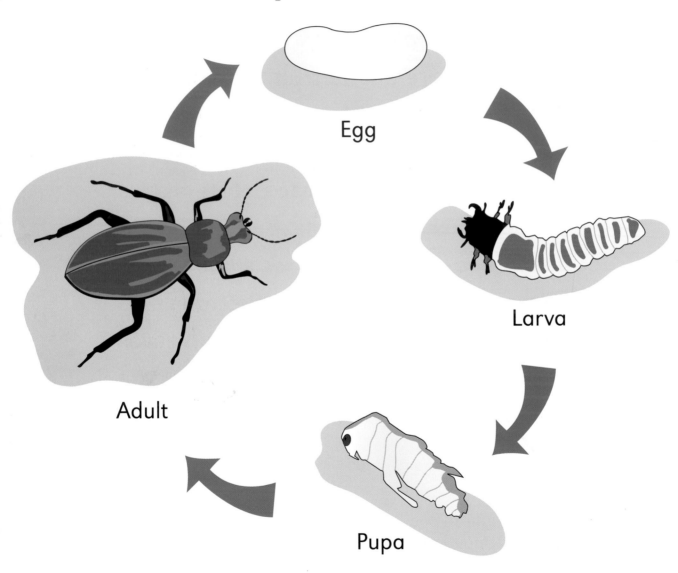

Egg

Larva

Pupa

Adult

Eggs and Larvae

All beetles begin as eggs. Beetle eggs can be different colors and shapes. Often they are round and smooth. Female beetles lay eggs one at a time or in groups. A **larva** forms inside each egg. Most larvae hatch after a few weeks or months.

Some larvae are called grubs. They are white and soft. They grow and shed their exoskeleton, or **molt**. A larva can molt seven times before becoming a **pupa**. Most larvae become pupae after a few weeks or months.

Pupae and Adults

During the pupal stage, beetles are changing into adults. They don't eat or walk. The pupal stage may last for a few days or all winter. Pupae become adults when they break out of the pupal skin.

Most beetles live only one year. Once beetles become adults, they only have a few weeks left to live.

◄ No longer a pupa, this adult ladybird beetle leaves its pupal skin. Ladybird beetles are also called ladybugs.

Dangers to Beetles

Many animals eat beetles. Birds, bats, mice, spiders, and even people eat beetles. Beetles sometimes kill and eat each other.

Beetles protect themselves in many ways. Some make chemicals that smell or taste bad. Others make noises to scare enemies.

Beetles face dangers everyday. Still, there are billions of beetles. Large numbers of these insects will continue to live worldwide.

◄ A Japanese beetle is wrapped up and will soon become a meal for a black and yellow garden spider.

Amazing Facts about Beetles

- Dung beetles shape animal waste into balls. They roll and bury the balls. In one night, a dung beetle can bury 250 times its own weight.

- Goliath beetles are some of the world's largest insects. They are about the size of a closed hand. A Goliath beetle weighs about as much as a tennis ball.

- Fireflies are beetles that make light. They flash their light on and off to find mates.

◄ A dung beetle rolls away a ball of waste. Later, beetle larvae and adults will eat the ball.

Glossary

abdomen (AB-duh-muhn)—the end section of an insect's body

antenna (an-TEN-uh)—a feeler on an insect's head

exoskeleton (eks-oh-SKE-luh-tuhn)—the hard outer covering of an insect

fungi (FUHN-jye)—organisms that have no leaves, flowers, or roots; mushrooms and molds are fungi.

larva (LAR-vuh)—an insect at the stage after an egg; more than one larva are larvae.

molt (MOHLT)—to shed an outer layer of skin, or exoskeleton, so a new exoskeleton can be seen.

pupa (PYOO-puh)—an insect at the stage of development between a larva and an adult; more than one pupa are pupae.

thorax (THOR-aks)—the middle section of an insect's body

Read More

Claybourne, Anna. *Beetles and Other Bugs.* Amazing Bugs. North Mankato, Minn.: Stargazer Books, 2004.

Derzipilski, Kathleen. *Beetles.* Animals, Animals. New York: Benchmark Books, 2004.

Internet Sites

FactHound offers a safe, fun way to find Internet sites related to this book. All of the sites on FactHound have been researched by our staff.

Here's how:
1. Visit *www.facthound.com*
2. Type in this special code **073683706X** for age-appropriate sites. Or enter a search word related to this book for a more general search.
3. Click on the **Fetch It** button.

FactHound will fetch the best sites for you!

Index